# Help the
# Bluefin Tuna

## by Grace Hansen

Abdo Kids Jumbo is an Imprint of Abdo Kids
abdobooks.com

**abdobooks.com**

Published by Abdo Kids, a division of ABDO, P.O. Box 398166, Minneapolis, Minnesota 55439.
Copyright © 2019 by Abdo Consulting Group, Inc. International copyrights reserved in all countries.
No part of this book may be reproduced in any form without written permission from the publisher.
Abdo Kids Jumbo™ is a trademark and logo of Abdo Kids.

102018

012019

 THIS BOOK CONTAINS RECYCLED MATERIALS

Photo Credits: Alamy, Getty Images, iStock, National Geographic Creative, Seapics.com, Shutterstock

Production Contributors: Teddy Borth, Jennie Forsberg, Grace Hansen

Design Contributors: Dorothy Toth, Laura Mitchell

Library of Congress Control Number: 2018946051

Publisher's Cataloging-in-Publication Data

Names: Hansen, Grace, author.

Title: Help the bluefin tuna / by Grace Hansen.

Description: Minneapolis, Minnesota : Abdo Kids, 2019 | Series: Little activists:
    endangered species | Includes glossary, index and online resources (page 24).

Identifiers: ISBN 9781532181993 (lib. bdg.) | ISBN 9781532182976 (ebook) |
    ISBN 9781532183461 (Read-to-me ebook)

Subjects: LCSH: Bluefin tuna--Juvenile literature. | Wildlife recovery--Juvenile
    literature. | Endangered species--Juvenile literature. | Overfishing--Juvenile
    literature.

Classification: DDC 333.954--dc23

# Table of Contents

## Bluefin Tuna

There are three species of Bluefin tuna. Atlantic, Pacific, and Southern Bluefin live in the world's oceans.

4

Bluefin tuna are built like 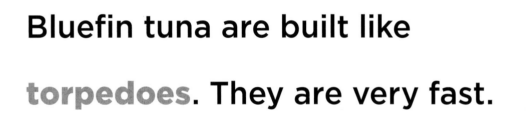 **torpedoes**. They are very fast.

6

Bluefin tuna can live between 15 and 30 years. They can grow to be 1,500 pounds (680.4 kg)!

9

## Status

In the last few decades, the Bluefin tuna has lost more than 90% of its population. Today, they are considered **endangered**.

## Threats

The population drop is due to overfishing. Bluefin tuna meat is in high demand.

13

Many Bluefins are caught

when they are too young.

They have not had time to

**spawn** and lay eggs.

A Bluefin tuna can lay millions of eggs each year. But very few of those eggs will hatch and survive. Those that do must be protected.

16

## Why They Matter

Bluefin tuna are good hunters. They are top **predators** in the ocean. They keep marine life balanced.

18

Bluefin tuna **migrate** thousands of miles each year. This makes it very hard to protect them. Many countries must come together to stop overfishing.

# Bluefin Tuna Overview

- Status: **Endangered**

- Population: Around 1.6 million Pacific Bluefin tuna (145,000 of which are reproducing adults)

- Habitat: Pacific, Atlantic, and Indian Oceans

- Greatest Threats: Overfishing and illegal fishing

# Glossary

**endangered** – in danger of becoming extinct.

**migrate** – to move from one place to another.

**predator** – an animal that hunts other animals for food.

**spawn** – to make a large number of eggs.

**species** – a group of living things that look alike and can have babies together.

**torpedo** – a long missile that is shaped like a cigar and is used to destroy ships.

# Index

**Abdo Kids**
ONLINE
FREE! ONLINE MULTIMEDIA RESOURCES

Visit **abdokids.com** and use this code to access crafts, games, videos, and more!

Abdo Kids Code:
**LHK1993**